Russell Westbrook

The amazing story of Russell Westbrook – one of basketball's most incredible players!

Table of Contents

Introduction

Congratulations for taking the time to read this book, documenting the incredible life and career of Russell Westbrook.

Followers of the NBA know Russell Westbrook as one of the biggest stars in professional basketball today. But his life and beginnings are highly interesting to read about and can serve as an inspiration for your own endeavors in life. It is often too easy to look at the success of athletes and other notable celebrities and forget to see where they came from. Often, their journeys to success provide insight and valuable lessons that can be applied by anyone.

In this book, you will read about the early life of Russell Westbrook, his high school and college playing days, his beginnings as an NBA player, and his various achievements as one of the league's most versatile stars. You will also read about other facets of his life and where he may be headed in the next few years.

Once again, thank you for choosing this book, and I hope you pick up some great lessons from the life of Russell Westbrook.

Chapter 1: Early Years

Russell Westbrook III was born in Long Beach, California on November 12, 1988 to Russell Westbrook, Jr. and Shannon Horton. His family lived in Long Beach for a few years after he was born, but later relocated to Hawthorne and then Torrance, also in California. Russell's father was passionate about basketball and was the one who taught him to play the sport at a young age. Russell and his younger brother, Raynard, would regularly play and go through basketball drills with their father.

One of the most notable stories about Russell Westbrook's early years is his friendship with Khelcey Barrs. Westbrook and Barrs were inseparable as teammates and friends in Lawndale, playing for Leuzinger High School. The two best friends planned on continuing to play together in college at UCLA. However, the possibility of ending up as college teammates became more and more remote, especially as Barrs received scholarship offers from colleges all around the United States.

Barrs had become a high school basketball sensation in 2003 when he led the Leuzinger High School basketball team to a shocking win over Long Beach Poly during the CIF Southern Section quarterfinals. Barrs was averaging 18 points, 11 boards, and three blocks per game in his sophomore year. While Barrs was being contacted by big names at the collegiate level, Westbrook had only heard back from a handful of smaller schools. Still, this did not deter the two buddies from enjoying their playing time together.

Their plan, however, was changed dramatically that year during a pickup game at L.A. Southwest College. Westbrook and Barrs were enjoying a spirited game with friends and teammates when Barrs suddenly collapsed on the court. He was rushed to nearby Centinela Hospital Medical Center in Inglewood, where he was pronounced dead due to an enlarged heart. Instead of an afternoon basketball game that Saturday, the 15-year-old Westbrook would be attending his best friend's funeral at Grace United Methodist Church, and his life changed dramatically.

After the sudden demise of his best friend, Westbrook decided to give more of an effort to becoming a better basketball player, as if he were now playing not just for himself but also for Barrs. He practiced his all-around skills and devoted more of his time to honing his game. Westbrook also took up some of the responsibilities left behind by his best friend, such as taking the trash out for Barrs' grandmother, who lived across the street from them.

Although sports took up a lot of his time, Westbrook's mother still made sure that it did not distract from his studies, and he did very well as far as academics. Westbrook was an honor student even though he was busy training hard, improving his game, and playing high school basketball for Leuzinger.

From his entry as a 5'8 freshman on the team, Westbrook underwent a growth spurt and was 5'10 by the time he was a junior, and he trained even harder, earning a spot on the starting line-up of the team. By the time he was a senior, Westbrook had reached a height of 6'2, and at 180 lbs, he was a formidable point guard. Westbrook became one of the cornerstones of the varsity team, averaging 25 points per game.

Westbrook always looks back at the loss of his best friend as a turning point in his life. To this day, he feels that he is playing for Barrs in a way, and stays in contact with his friend's family.

After the death of Barrs, Westbrook realized the brevity of life and how quickly it could end, so he wanted to take hold of every opportunity given to him, without questioning his ability to reach for his dreams. Westbrook had a goal of becoming the best point guard out there, and he was out to prove his naysayers or doubters wrong.

In his senior year at Leuzinger, Westbrook averaged 25.1 points, 8.7 rebounds, 3.1 steals, and 2.3 assists per game, leading the school to a 25-4 win-loss record. Also in his senior year, Westbrook had 14 double-double games, scored at least 30 points in eight different games, and scored a career-high 51 points on January 6, 2006 against Carson.

With this stellar senior year performance, Westbrook caught the attention of UCLA head coach Ben Howland, who recruited him to play for the UCLA Bruins. Thus, his dream of playing for UCLA with his best friend Barrs was partially fulfilled. After graduation, Westbrook headed for college.

Chapter Summary

• Russell Westbrook III was born on November 12, 1988 in Long Beach, California to Russell Westbrook, Jr. and Shannon Horton.

• Much of his childhood was spent in Hawthorne and Torrance, California.

• Russell and his younger brother learned to play basketball from their father.

• Russell's best friend, Khelcey Barrs, was a rising high school basketball star being recruited by major colleges before his untimely death at the age of 16. He died during a pickup game due to an enlarged heart.

• After Barrs' death, Russell trained extra hard and vowed to play for both of them, and fulfil their dream of playing for UCLA.

• Westbrook played for Leuzinger High School. In his junior year, he was chosen to play in the starting line-up.

• As a senior at Leuzinger, Westbrook was scoring 25.1 points per game, getting about 8.7 rebounds, and adding 3.1 steals and 2.3 assists per game.

• He scored a career-high 51 points against Carson on January 6, 2006.

• Westbrook caught the eye of Ben Howland, the head coach of UCLA, and he was recruited to play for the Bruins.

Chapter 2: College

Not a lot of big-name college basketball programs in the United States took notice of Westbrook during his time playing for Leuzinger High School. This changed, however, when UCLA Bruins head coach Ben Howland recruited Westbrook to play for the school. This occurred after Bruins standout Jordan Farmar announced that he was joining the NBA draft, leaving UCLA in need of a new point guard.

At the time, Farmar was one of the key players of the Bruins, and the talented point guard led the Bruins to the National Championship game during the 2006 NCAA Tournament, where they lost the title to the Florida Gators. Farmar then declared for the NBA Draft on April 20, 2006. Coach Howland decided to offer a scholarship to Westbrook, knowing he could soon fill the void left behind by Farmar.

Westbrook was given the jersey number 0 the whole time he played for the UCLA Bruins. As a freshman, he came off the bench after Darren Collison, and was mostly utilized as a defender and second-stringer. He averaged 3.4 points, 0.8 rebounds, and 0.7 assists in his first year with the Bruins. Westbrook averaged only nine minutes per game as a freshman, and he needed to work on a lot of aspects of his game, particularly his shooting. Westbrook put in the time and spent hours practicing and honing his skills.

By the time he was a sophomore, Westbrook had transformed himself into an expert in defense, assists, and dunking. Westbrook mostly played as a 2-guard, forming the Bruins backcourt with Collison, and Westbrook averaged 12.7 points and 4 assists per game. UCLA reached the NCAA tournament as the top-seeded team from the West, and were heavily favored to win the national championship. During the second round of the tournament, playing against Texas A&M, Westbrook dunked the ball right at the buzzer, but the basket was waived off because apparently, he was in the air too long and the ball was in his hands at the time the buzzer sounded.

Westbrook's decision to wear the number 0 would garner attention and introduce his fashion sense to a bigger audience. When featured by the New York Times regarding the growing trend of players who chose to wear the number 0, Westbrook would explain that it helped him to gain his swag in the game. "You go with the zero when you've been through something and you are looking to get a new beginning," he said.

His two seasons with UCLA were relatively successful as the Bruins reached the Final Four both years. In 2007, they faced Florida but lost 76-66, with Florida eventually going on to win the national title. The following year, in the national semi-final game, the UCLA Bruins faced Memphis, who were led by Derrick Rose. Westbrook led the Bruins with 22 points, but they lost to Memphis 78-63.

A comparison between Westbrook's freshman and sophomore year statistics with UCLA would clearly show how he improved his game, especially when Collison was sidelined with an injury and Westbrook became part of the starting five. His first-year statistics were 3.4 points per game, 0.4 steals per game, 0.8 blocks per game, 0.7 assists per game, 45.7% field goals, 40.9% three-point shots, and 54.8% from the free throw line. In contrast, the following year, Westbrook averaged 12.7 points per game, 1.6 steals per game, 4.3 assists per game, 46.5% field goals, and 71.3% from the free throw line. As a sophomore, he was also awarded Pac-10 Defensive Player of the Year and named to the All-Pac-10 Third Team.

After two years with the Bruins, Westbrook declared for the 2008 NBA Draft. It would be the start of his exciting and highly impressive career as a professional basketball player.

Chapter Summary

• Westbrook was recruited by UCLA Bruins head coach Ben Howland with the hopes that he would fill in the void left by Jordan Farmar.

• As a freshman, Westbrook came off the bench after Darren Collison, and only averaged nine minutes per game.

• Westbrook worked on his game, especially his shooting skills, and in his sophomore year became part of the Bruins starting lineup after Collison was injured.

• The UCLA Bruins reached the Final Four both years that Westbrook played for the team.

• After his sophomore year, Westbrook announced his decision to join the NBA Draft.

Chapter 3: Entering The NBA

The 2008 NBA Draft featured 39 collegiate players and five international players who were considered early-entry candidates, aside from those who were automatically eligible for the draft. It was held at Madison Square Garden's Washington Mutual Theatre on June 26, 2008, with the Chicago Bulls, Miami Heat, and Minnesota Timberwolves getting the first three selections.

The 2008 Draft was notable because it featured several names that would become some of the league's biggest superstars to date. Derrick Rose of the University of Memphis was the first overall pick drafted by Chicago, with Michael Beasley becoming the second overall pick, and O.J. Mayo being selected third overall. All of the first three draft picks that season were freshmen, a first in NBA draft history.

Another notable story in the 2008 NBA Draft was the final appearance of the Seattle SuperSonics as a franchise. Soon after the draft, the franchise moved to Oklahoma City and became known as the Oklahoma City Thunder. It was the Seattle SuperSonics/Oklahoma City Thunder who drafted Russell Westbrook fourth overall, paving the way for his professional career in the NBA. On July 5, 2008, Westbrook officially signed with the Thunder, along with DJ White, who was originally drafted by the Detroit Pistons before being traded.

Scouting reports for Westbrook prior to the draft in 2008 were mixed. Some writers believed he should stay with UCLA and finish out his four years. One writer described Westbrook as a player who "knows his limitations and has no problem fitting in and being just another cog." In the DraftExpress report, Westbrook was compared to Leandro Barbosa. He was also described by experts as a prolific defensive stopper and an off-the-bench spark.

Westbrook was at the right place at just the opportune time, as the SuperSonics/Thunder were sort of in limbo. Aside from the transition of relocating from Seattle to Oklahoma City, the franchise needed a player who could support its main man

Kevin Durant. Durant needed someone to take some pressure off of him in the backcourt, and to rely on for additional scoring. General Manager Sam Presti initially wanted to trade their fourth draft selection, but he was unable to iron out any deals with other teams, so the franchise decided to take a risk and pick Westbrook. It turned out to be an excellent decision.

In his rookie season with the Thunder, Westbrook had averages of 15.3 points, 5.3 assists, 4.9 rebounds, and 1.3 steals per game. A notable achievement during his rookie season was his very first triple-double performance of his career, which he recorded on March 2, 2009. Westbrook was the first rookie since Chris Paul to record a triple-double performance, and only the third rookie in franchise history to achieve this (the other two being Art Harris and Gary Payton).

That season was challenging for the Thunder, however, with a woeful 3-29 regular season start. Although Durant was putting in an impressive 25-point scoring average per game, and Westbrook was also contributing very well, there was no on-court chemistry yet between the two players.

That season, Westbrook was selected to be part of the NBA All-Rookie First Team, and he finished fourth in the 2008-09 Rookie of the Year voting. Derrick Rose led all candidates, followed by O.J. Mayo and Brook Lopez. However, the Thunder failed to make it to the NBA playoffs during Westbrook's rookie year.

In his second year in the NBA, Westbrook became a full-time starter for the Oklahoma City Thunder. He averaged 16.1 points, 8.0 assists, 4.9 boards, and 1.3 steals per game. Westbrook made 10 points and dished out a career-best 16 assists on April 4, 2010 in a win against the Minnesota Timberwolves, 116-108. It was a much better season performance for the Thunder as they finished with a 50-32 record, more than doubling their number of wins from the previous season. The franchise qualified for the NBA Playoffs, but were tasked to face the Los Angeles Lakers in the first round.

In his very first playoff series, Westbrook registered impressive numbers, garnering 20.5 points, 6 rebounds, 6 assists, and 3.2 steals per game. The Thunder squad of Durant, James Harden,

Serge Ibaka, and Westbrook made a splash nationally and gave Kobe Bryant and his team a run for their money. Oklahoma City even pulled off two wins against the mighty Los Angeles team. The Lakers proved too strong for the Thunder, however, and Oklahoma City bowed out in the first round. The Lakers would go on to win the national title that year.

That first playoff experience would ignite a different level of play from the Thunder, and Westbrook and the others on the team suddenly found a way to compliment each other and become title contenders. The following season would see an even more formidable Russell Westbrook taking his place and rising as a bona fide basketball superstar.

Chapter Summary

• Russell Westbrook was part of the 2008 NBA Draft, where he was selected fourth overall by the Seattle SuperSonics. The franchise moved to Oklahoma shortly thereafter and was rebranded as the Oklahoma City Thunder.

• In the same year, Derrick Rose was the first overall pick, followed by Michael Beasley, and O.J. Mayo.

• Westbrook was picked by the Thunder partly because they needed someone to support Kevin Durant in the backcourt.

• In his rookie year, Westbrook had respectable averages, and he recorded his first career triple-double on March 2, 2009.

• In his second year in the NBA, Westbrook ramped up his averages and officially became a starter for the Thunder. The team finished strong and qualified for the playoffs.

• Oklahoma City's line-up of Durant, Westbrook, Harden, and Ibaka became a sensation in the playoffs, although they lost the series to eventual champions, the Los Angeles Lakers.

Chapter 4: The Rising Of Russell Westbrook

Before the start of the 2010-11 NBA season, Westbrook was selected to join the United States team in the FIBA World Championships held in Istanbul, Turkey. Westbrook joined his teammate, Kevin Durant, along with Derrick Rose, Chauncey Billups, Rudy Gay, Andre Iguodala, Stephen Curry, Kevin Love, Lamar Odom, Tyson Chandler, Eric Gordon, and Danny Granger in the lineup. The selection did not include any holdovers from the 2008 men's basketball team which won the Olympic gold, and it was a relatively smaller lineup than previous fielded squads.

During the tournament, Westbrook proved to be a consistent and reliable addition to the US selection, playing an average of 19.4 minutes per game and contributing 9.1 points, 2.6 assists, and 2.8 rebounds per game. He was among the top five on the team in minutes played per game, and also among the top for scoring and assists. Team USA swept all nine games and won their first World Championship title since 1994, automatically earning the United States a spot in the London 2012 Olympics. Team USA also passed Argentina to reclaim the top world ranking.

Back from the FIBA World Championship, the 2010-11 NBA season saw an improved performance from Westbrook throughout the year. He scored 43 big points against the Indiana Pacers on November 26, 2010 in an overtime win over the Pacers, 110-106. At the time, this was Westbrook's career-best in scoring. Just a few days later, on December 1st, Westbrook had 38 points, 9 assists, and a career-best 15 rebounds against the New Jersey Nets in a triple-overtime victory. Westbrook's regular season averages were 21.9 points per game, 8.2 assists per game, 4.6 rebounds per game, and 1.9 steals per game.

His teammate, Durant, described Westbrook's experience playing with Team USA as an important transition point for him. "He's always had confidence, but I think playing in USA games really pushed it over the top," Durant remarked. Sure enough, analysts commented that Westbrook seemed comfortable blending in with players he had grown up watching on television, and showed little nervousness stepping up his game.

His stellar performance earned him the nod of NBA head coaches who selected Westbrook as a Western Conference reserve player for the 2011 NBA All-Star Game held in Los Angeles, California. At the time of the selection, Westbrook was the only NBA player averaging 22 points, 8 assists, and 5 boards each game. Considering he was a point guard, the numbers were indeed impressive. Other players who were selected for the Western Conference reserve team included Blake Griffin, Deron Williams, Dirk Nowitzki, Tim Duncan, Manu Ginobili, and Pau Gasol.

Westbrook was also named to the All-NBA Second Time for the very first time in his professional career. Another milestone for Westbrook during this season was scoring his 4,000th NBA career point, which he achieved against the Detroit Pistons on March 11, 2011. He joined an elite group of only five players in the history of the NBA who recorded 4,000 points, 1,500 assists, and 1,000 rebounds within their first three years playing in the league.

The Oklahoma City Thunder advanced to the playoffs once again after a 55-27 win-loss record at the end of the regular season. In the first round of the playoffs, the Thunder faced the Denver Nuggets and finished the series in five games. Next, they were up against the Memphis Grizzlies, a team that was coming off a shocking upset over the top-seed San Antonio Spurs in six games. The Thunder-Grizzlies series went the distance, and in the seventh game, Westbrook contributed a triple-double performance, which, along with Durant's massive 39-point output, was enough to put the Thunder over the edge and reach the Western Conference Finals.

In the Western Conference Finals, the Thunder squared off versus the Dallas Mavericks. The Mavs were well-rested heading into the series, having finished off the defending champions, the Los Angeles Lakers, in a four-game sweep which gave them eight days of rest. The Thunder, on the other hand, were coming off a seven-game series which had been physically and mentally challenging. Oklahoma City could only muster one win against Dallas, and the Mavericks won the series at home in a 100-96 victory on May 25, 2011. Dallas would go on to win the NBA title that year.

With their playoff run, the Thunder continued to rise in popularity, with television ratings for Thunder games within the OKC market setting new records. Westbrook's stellar performance in the playoffs, with averages of 23.8 points per game, 6.4 assists per game, and 5.4 rebounds per game, cemented his standing as one of the fast-rising NBA stars to watch out for.

The fourth lockout in the history of the NBA occurred in 2011 and lasted for 161 days from July 1 to December 8. Thus, the 2011-12 NBA regular season was delayed until Christmas Day, and the season was shortened to 66 games from its regular 82 games. As the season resumed, Westbrook continued putting in impressive performances, including a 45-point output against the Minnesota Timberwolves on March 23, 2012. The Thunder won in double overtime, 149-140.

Throughout the lockout-shortened regular season, Westbrook averaged 23.6 points per game, 5.5 assists per game, 4.6 rebounds per game, and 1.7 steals per game. For the second straight year, Westbrook was picked by coaches for the 2012 NBA All-Star Game, and he was also voted to the All-NBA Second Team. Westbrook was Western Conference Player of the Week for both January 23-29, and February 6-12.

The Thunder finished the regular season with a 47-19 win-loss slate and earned the second seed in the Western Conference behind the San Antonio Spurs heading into the playoffs. Oklahoma City once again faced the Dallas Mavericks in the first round of the playoffs, but this time, the Thunder won the series in convincing fashion against the Mavericks, sweeping the defending champions. Westbrook led all Thunder players in scoring in the first two games of the series, with 28 points in Game 1, and 29 points in Game 2.

In the next round, the Thunder faced the Los Angeles Lakers. Westbrook again led the OKC squad in scoring in several games of the series, with 27 points scored in Game 1, 37 points in Game 4, and 28 points in the deciding Game 5. The Thunder disposed of the Lakers 4-1 to advance to the Western Conference Finals.

In the conference finals, Oklahoma City squared off against the powerhouse San Antonio Spurs. The Spurs won the first two outings at the AT&T Center in San Antonio, before the Thunder regained their footing and won the next four games, powered by explosive outputs from Durant in the scoring department. Westbrook had 9 assists in Game 3, 12 assists in Game 5, and another 5 assists in Game 6, and helped propel the Thunder to a convincing 4-2 series win and the franchise's first NBA Finals appearance since the transition from the Seattle SuperSonics.

The 2012 NBA Finals started on June 12 with the Thunder having a home court advantage against the Miami Heat, led by LeBron James, Dwyane Wade, and Chris Bosh. OKC won Game 1 of the series 105-94. Instrumental to the win was Durant's 36 points and Westbrook's 11 assists. The Heat came back in Game 2 and won 100-96 to tie the series and deal the Thunder their first home playoff loss for that season. Miami would go on to the win the next three games and clinch the championship title.

Westbrook's NBA Finals debut was impressive particularly as he joined Michael Jordan as the only other player to score more than 25 points and 10 assists in their very first NBA Finals. Westbrook also scored 43 points, a career playoff best, in Game 4 of the series versus the Heat, although the Thunder still lost the game.

Westbrook would once again be given the chance to play for the United States in 2012, as he was selected for the 2012 US men's basketball team. Westbrook joined LeBron James, Carmelo Anthony, Deron Williams, Chris Paul, Kobe Bryant, Kevin Durant, Andre Iguodala, Tyson Chandler, Kevin Love, Rudy Gay, Anthony Davis, and James Harden. The US men's national basketball team won the Olympic gold, and it was Westbrook's second gold medal, the first one being the FIBA World Championship two years prior.

After the 2012 NBA Finals, the Thunder would undergo a major shake-up. Only a few days before the 2012-13 regular season kicked off, contract extension talks with James Harden bogged down, and he was traded to the Houston Rockets.

Despite the loss of key player Harden, the Thunder soldiered on during the 2012-13 regular season. Westbrook averaged 23.2 points, 5.2 rebounds, 1.8 steals, and 7.4 assists per game, as the Thunder finished the regular season with the top seed in the Western Conference, and another NBA Playoffs appearance.

It was during the first round of the playoffs against the Houston Rockets that Westbrook was sidelined by an injury. In the second game of the series, Westbrook and Rockets guard Patrick Beverley collided with each other as Beverley tried to steal the ball from Westbrook. Westbrook's right knee was injured in the incident, but although he was bothered by the pain, he continued to play in the game and scored 29 points. Tests the following day revealed a tear in his right meniscus, which required surgery. The surgery was done on April 27 of that year, and Westbrook did not return for the rest of the NBA Playoffs. The Thunder still went on to win the series versus the Rockets, but in the next round, they were eliminated by the Memphis Grizzlies in five games.

Due to the injury, Westbrook needed to undergo another surgery on his right knee. Before the start of the 2013-14 NBA season, the Thunder announced that Westbrook would not be able to join training camp or play in any preseason games, and he would likely miss up to six weeks of the regular season as well in order to recover from the surgery. In the announcement, General Manager Sam Presti described that while Westbrook was no longer experiencing pain and was recovering well from the first operation, there was some swelling that had not subsided, and consulting doctors had suggested the second procedure in order to alleviate the swelling and also increase Westbrook's chances of better long-term performance.

Westbrook was very disappointed with the outcome, especially with the prospect of missing the first few weeks of the regular season. Despite the adversity, the star would once again show amazing resilience, and return to the court in high style.

<u>**Chapter Summary**</u>

• Russell Westbrook played for the 2010 US men's basketball team in the FIBA World Championships, and the 2012 US Olympic men's basketball team, winning a gold medal with each selection.

• Westbrook's experience playing in the 2010 FIBA World Championship has been credited as among the most crucial in his early years in the NBA, boosting his confidence and level of play.

• Westbrook was selected by NBA head coaches to join the Western Conference team in the 2011 NBA All-Star Game.

• Westbrook's star continued to rise during the lockout-protracted 2011-12 NBA season, as he was named Western Conference Player of the Week twice. The Thunder brushed off the Dallas Mavericks, the Los Angeles Lakers, and the San Antonio Spurs in the NBA Playoffs to reach the NBA Finals versus the Miami Heat.

• After their Finals loss to the Heat, the Thunder traded James Harden to the Rockets. Westbrook needed to step up his play further and he delivered with impressive averages.

• A knee surgery during the first round of the 2013 Playoffs ended Westbrook's season; he also missed training camp and preseason games before the next NBA regular season.

Chapter 5: Fighting Back From Injury

The prognosis was that Russell Westbrook would miss at least the first two weeks of the 2013-14 NBA regular season as he recovered from the right knee injury. However, Westbrook surprised everyone when he suited up on November 3 versus the Phoenix Suns, sitting out only the first two regular season games of the season. Then, on Christmas day, 2013 in a game against the New York Knicks, Westbrook did not just play through the injury, but he did so in the most dominating fashion.

Westbrook scored 14 points and added 13 rebounds and 10 assists in Oklahoma City's 123-94 thrashing of New York. It would go down in history as the most dominant win by a road team in any Christmas Day game in NBA history, and Westbrook's triple-double output was only the eighth triple-double for an NBA Christmas Day game ever. It would also be the seventh triple-double performance in his career.

The following day, the Thunder announced that Westbrook would need to have arthroscopic surgery on his right knee and would likely be out at least until after the All-Star festivities. Before the announcement, Westbrook was contributing 21.3 points per game, 7 assists per game, and 6 rebounds per game for the Thunder, averaging 32.9 playing minutes.

Thunder head coach Scott Brooks acknowledged that Westbrook would be sorely missed by the team during his absence, but kept an optimistic outlook. "Obviously we are a very good team with him, and without him we're still going to be a very good team," Brooks said.

Fortunately for the Thunder, the team remained very competitive even through Westbrook's injury absence as Durant and the rest of the team stepped up. Finally, Westbrook was cleared to play on February 20, 2014, albeit playing only limited minutes per game and usually resting on the second night of back-to-back scheduled games.

Where other players would have taken longer to regain their form, Westbrook showed a remarkable ability to get back in sync. On March 4, 2014, or less than a month since being cleared to play again, he logged his second triple-double performance of the season, this time against the Philadelphia 76ers. Westbrook scored 13 points, had 10 boards, and dished 14 assists in a span of 20 minutes as the Thunder roared to a 125-92 win over the 76ers. This went down in history as the second fastest recorded triple-double performance in league history, surpassed only by Jim Tucker of the Syracuse Nationals who recorded a triple-double within 17 minutes back in 1955. At the end of the regular season, Westbrook averaged 32.9 minutes played per game, shot 42.4% from the field, 31.8% beyond the arc, 79.3% from the free throw line, and averaged 21.9 points, 1.8 steals, 6.9 assists, and 5.7 rebounds per game for Oklahoma City.

At the close of the regular season, the Thunder had a 59-23 win-loss record, and the second seed in the Western Conference. In the first round, Oklahoma City faced the Memphis Grizzlies in a thrilling seven-game series, then took care of the Los Angeles Clippers in the second round, 4-2. The Western Conference Finals saw the Thunder going up against the dominant San Antonio Spurs. The Thunder came up short, losing to the Spurs in six games, and San Antonio eventually won the NBA championship against the Miami Heat.

During the postseason, Westbrook posted averages of 26.7 points, 8.1 assists, and 7.3 rebounds per game, including an explosive Game 4 performance against the Spurs in the Western Conference Finals where he recorded 40 points, 10 assists, 5 rebounds, and 5 steals. In NBA history, only Michael Jordan has been able to log those statistics in a playoff game.

Yet another injury would side line Westbrook early in the 2014-15 regular season, as he suffered a small fracture of the second metacarpal of his right hand in a game versus the Los Angeles Clippers. The injury came only a couple of days after a 38-point explosion by Westbrook in their season-opening game against the Portland Trail Blazers. In a stroke of bad luck, his teammate Kevin Durant was also out with a foot injury which happened over the preseason, and was not expected to back for six to eight weeks.

The Oklahoma City Thunder struggled without Westbrook and Durant in the early goings of the season, and the franchise had a 4-12 record when Westbrook suited up on November 28 versus the New York Knicks. In his comeback game, he led OKC with 32 points, and the Thunder overpowered the Knicks. In the next game against the New Orleans Pelicans, Durant also returned from injury, and the Thunder sprang to life once again, winning seven games in a row and getting back to playoff contender status.

Westbrook logged another triple-double performance, the ninth in his career, on January 16, 2015, this time against the Golden State Warriors. His 17 points, 15 boards, and 17 assists (best in his career) propelled the Thunder to a convincing 127-115 victory over the Warriors. February saw Westbrook reaching even more career milestones, as he dropped 45 points against the New Orleans Pelicans, before later breaking that record with a new career-high 48 points versus the same team.

The 2015 All-Star Game saw the return of Westbrook to the annual star-studded exhibition game after missing the previous year's game due to his injury. Westbrook scored 41 points in the All-Star Game and was voted the All-Star MVP. 27 of those points were scored in 11 minutes of the first half of the game, which became a new record for the All-Star Game, and only Wilt Chamberlain's 42-point record in 1962 surpasses Westbrook's performance.

After the All-Star festivities, Westbrook's electrifying performance in the regular season continued, as he dropped 21 points and 17 assists versus the Denver Nuggets, then logged three straight triple-double performances against the Denver Nuggets, Indiana Pacers, and Portland Trail Blazers. As February closed, Westbrook was getting impressive averages of 31.2 points, 9.1 rebounds, and 10.3 assists per game.

As if this was not enough, Westbrook logged 49 points, 16 boards, and 10 assists on March 4 versus the Philadelphia 76ers for his fourth consecutive triple-double. Not only did this performance contribute heavily to Oklahoma City's 123-118 overtime win against Philadelphia, it would also put Westbrook in the record books as the first NBA player since Michael Jordan to have four consecutive triple-doubles. Towards the end of the regular season, he recorded eleven more triple-double performances as the Thunder furiously fought to make it to the postseason. However, Oklahoma City fell short of the goal, and missed the playoffs despite a respectable 45-37 win-loss slate.

With the injury now fully behind him, Westbrook continued to post big numbers for the Oklahoma City Thunder in the 2015-16 NBA regular season. In the Thunder's season-opening game against the San Antonio Spurs, Westbrook led all scorers with 33 points, and the Thunder prevailed over the Spurs 112-106. Westbrook and Durant masterfully led the Thunder two nights later against the Orlando Magic, as Westbrook scored 48, and Durant had 43 points. The game went into double-overtime with Oklahoma City emerging on top, 139-136.

In a game against the Washington Wizards on November 10, 2015, Westbrook logged 22 points, 11 assists, and 11 rebounds; his first triple-double for the season, and then came back the next game and had another triple-double performance (21 points, 17 rebounds, 11 assists) against the Philadelphia 76ers.

His on-court chemistry with Durant continued to grow as they would combine explosive performances and lead the Thunder to convincing victories, including a December 27 win versus the Denver Nuggets where Westbrook and Durant became the first teammates to both score at least 25 points and 10 assists in a regular season game, with the last pair being John Stockton and Karl Malone of the Utah Jazz back in 1996. Westbrook and Durant were named the Western Conference's Co-Players of the Month of December because of their stellar achievements.

The NBA All-Star Game of 2016 saw the very first time when Westbrook was voted to be part of the starting lineup. He tallied 31 points, 8 rebounds, 5 steals, and 5 assists in just 22 minutes of playing time, earning him his second consecutive All-Star MVP Award, and leading the Western Conference to a 196-173 win over the Eastern Conference.

Westbrook became only the fourth player in league history to score at least 15 points, 15 assists, five steals, and five rebounds in one game, when he logged 16 points, 15 assists, 8 rebounds, and 5 steals in a January 20, 2016 game versus the Charlotte

Hornets. In the month of March, Westbrook would tally six triple-double performances, the highest by any NBA player in one calendar month since Michael Jordan's seven triple-doubles in April of 1989. Westbrook would go on to tally his 18th triple-double for the season against the Los Angeles Lakers on April 11, and tie Magic Johnson's record for most triple-doubles in one season.

After the regular season, the Thunder had a 55-27 win-loss record, the third-best in the Western Conference, and enough to book a first round playoff series against the Dallas Mavericks. In Game 1, Westbrook led all Thunder scorers with 24 points and 11 assists as Oklahoma City took the win. Dallas could only muster a Game 2 win, before the Thunder took the next three games to win the series outright. In the deciding Game 5, Westbrook led the Thunder with 36 points, 12 boards, and 9 assists.

In the next round, the Thunder again faced Western Conference powerhouse San Antonio. The Spurs took Game 1 and 3, while the Thunder overpowered them in Game 2 and the final three games of the series to win the conference semi-finals, 4-2. Throughout the series, Westbrook led the Thunder in assists per game, with as much as 15 assists in Game 4.

The Western Conference Finals pitted the Thunder against the surging Golden State Warriors. Westbrook contributed big points in the tightly-contested series, including 27 points in their Game 1 win, and 36 points in their Game 4 victory as the Thunder went up 3-1 over the Warriors. He added 22 rebounds and 11 assists in that game to log his fifth playoff triple-double. But it was in the assists department that Westbrook would really show his contribution, leading all Oklahoma City players throughout the series.

It looked as if the Thunder would march right into the NBA Finals as they took a commanding 3-1 lead over the Warriors. But the Warriors managed to rally and win three straight games to win the series in the seventh game. In Game 7, Oklahoma City gained a 13-point advantage early in the game and a 6-point advantage at halftime but appeared to lose steam in the third quarter as the Warriors rallied back and eventually took the lead. The Thunder made a run in the fourth quarter, but it was not enough to overpower the Warriors as Golden State erased the 1-3 series deficit and won the game, 96-88.

The series would be the last time that NBA fans would see Durant in a Thunder jersey playing alongside Westbrook. After the postseason, a big move would rock the Oklahoma City franchise, with the responsibility of leading the team falling squarely on the shoulders of Westbrook.

Chapter Summary

• After his injury in 2013, Westbrook was not expected to return to play until after two weeks into the regular season. However, he only missed the first two games.

• In a Christmas Day game versus New York, Westbrook would log a triple-double performance, only the eighth by a player for an NBA Christmas Day game, and lead the Thunder to a dominant 123-94 victory.

• The next day, Oklahoma City announced that Westbrook would require arthroscopic surgery on his right knee. He was out until February 20, 2014.

• Soon after being cleared to play, Westbrook would only play limited minutes and rest on the second of back-to-back games.

• Less than one month after returning to play, Westbrook scored 13 points, 10 rebounds, and 14 assists, all in under 20 minutes.

• Despite being sidelined by injury for several weeks, Westbrook ended the season averaging decent numbers across the board, and the Thunder went as far as the Western Conference Finals, where they lost to the San Antonio Spurs.

• Westbrook struggled with another injury during the 2014-15 regular season, along with Kevin Durant. Although the Thunder furiously came back after Westbrook and Durant returned to play, it was not enough and Oklahoma City missed the playoffs.

• More triple-double performances became part of Westbrook's 2015-16 regular season. His record of 18 triple-doubles for the season tied the record held by Magic Johnson.

• A seven-game series against the Golden State Warriors in the 2016 Western Conference Finals saw the Thunder establishing a 3-1 lead, only to falter towards the end and lose the series to the Warriors.

Chapter 6: Russell Takes The Reins

During the NBA off-season of 2016, much speculations swirled around the Oklahoma City Thunder, particularly regarding Russell Westbrook's teammate, Kevin Durant. Durant was a free agent, and rumors were rife that he was setting his sights elsewhere after playing in Oklahoma City for nine years. Sure enough, one week after his free agency, and after lots of unconfirmed reports involving the San Antonio Spurs, Miami Heat, and Boston Celtics, Durant signed with the defending champion Golden State Warriors.

Incidentally, it was the Warriors that had eliminated the Thunder from the playoffs just the season prior to acquiring Durant. But as free agency set in and Golden State made a play for Durant, they had none other than head coach Steve Kerr and core players, Stephen Curry, Klay Thompson, and Draymond Green as part of the pitch to recruit Durant.

Durant's decision to leave the Thunder opened up trade speculation around Westbrook, especially as his contract was expiring the following year. With Durant's departure, the Thunder did not want to take any chances and wanted to make sure they were keeping Westbrook, so they offered a contract extension until the 2017-18 season. The contract extension also contained a player option, but with the opportunity for Westbrook to decline and instead opt for free agency as he reached the 10-year-veteran maximum pay.

In his statement soon after signing the agreement, Westbrook expressed his gratitude for the contract extension offer with the Thunder and indicated that he was looking forward to continue playing for the only NBA team he has played for. "I'm really excited about moving forward with this group of guys and continuing to play in front of the best fans in the world," he said.

With Durant gone, Westbrook needed to take charge for the Thunder, and sure enough, he stepped up to the challenge with strong numbers and steady leadership. On October 28, 2016, in Oklahoma City's second regular season game, Westbrook recorded 51 points, 13 rebounds, and 10 assists, marking the first time that a player had a 50-point triple-double since Kareem Abdul-Jabbar back in 1975. The feat helped the Thunder win over the Phoenix Suns in overtime, 113-110.

Westbrook would go on to set more triple-double records throughout the regular season, and he became part of an exclusive club of NBA players with two triple-doubles over the first three regular season games. Others who have achieved this are Magic Johnson, Oscar Robertson, and Jerry Lucas. Entering the month of December, Westbrook was already averaging a triple-double, and he had a seven-game triple-double streak which tied for Michael Jordan's record in 1989.
Halfway through the season, his averages were 30.8 points, 10.7 rebounds, and 10.5 assists per game. By the time the All-Star Weekend came along, his average was 31.1 points, 10.5 rebounds, and 10.1 assists per game. Westbrook's 21st triple-double of the regular season was against the Golden State Warriors on January 18, when the Thunder lost to former teammate Durant. Westbrook would also score his career-high 58 points against the Portland Trail Blazers on March 7, in a 126-121 loss.

Westbrook's impressive performance continued well after the All-Star break, and he joined Robertson as the only players in league history with triple-double averages for the whole season. Robertson held the record for most triple-doubles logged in a season, which stood at 41. This was obliterated by Westbrook on April 9 in a game against the Denver Nuggets. Westbrook had 50 points in the contest and scored the game-winning 36-foot buzzer-beater to clinch the win for the Thunder, 106-105. At the end of the regular season, the Thunder had a 47-35 win-loss record and the sixth seed in the Western Conference.

In the first round of the playoffs, Oklahoma City faced James Harden and the Houston Rockets. Westbrook would set yet another record, this time in Game 2 of the series as he scored 51 points, 13 assists, and 10 rebounds to log his sixth career playoff triple-double and the highest-scoring triple-double performance in NBA Playoffs history. Westbrook would log three consecutive playoff triple-double performances in this series, but it was not enough to prevail against the Rockets, and Houston won the series 4-1. Westbrook was selected as the NBA's Most Valuable Player at the NBA Awards Show on June 26, 2017.

With his remarkable performance, it was inevitable that Oklahoma City would do everything to keep him in their fold. Westbrook would be offered the biggest guaranteed contract ever in NBA history, starting with a five-year, $205 million contract extension, and a six-season deal worth $233 million which runs to 2023. The contract also included a player option for the 2022-23 season.

OKC Thunder Chairman Clayton I. Bennett described Westbrook as the epitome of everything their organization could hope for as they build a basketball team for the city. "His character, integrity, and relentless drive have been a great unifier that has deeply and positively affected the spirit of our fans inside our arena, in our classrooms, and in our neighborhoods," Bennett said.

Thunder Executive Vice President and General Manager Sam Presti was also profuse in his admiration for Westbrook. "We are extremely fortunate to have an athlete, competitor and person such as Russell wear the Thunder uniform," said Presti.

For his part, Westbrook reiterated that nothing has changed as far as his desire to continue playing for Oklahoma City. "When you play in Oklahoma City you play in front of the best fans in the world, I'm looking forward to bringing everything I've got, for them, this city and for this organization."

Indeed, Westbrook's contribution to Oklahoma City has extended beyond just his basketball skills and his leadership in the team. His influence has also expanded as he explores other interests and endeavors beyond just basketball. In the next chapter, you will read about some of these interests that take up Westbrook's time when he is not laying it all out on the basketball court.

<u>**Chapter Summary**</u>

• Russell Westbrook had to take over the leadership role within the Oklahoma City Thunder as his teammate Kevin Durant transferred to the Golden State Warriors prior to the start of the 2016-17 NBA season.

• After Durant's departure, the Thunder signed Westbrook to a contract extension through the 2018 season.

• Westbrook elevated his game to a whole new level, logging triple-double performances all throughout the regular season and tying or surpassing records set by NBA greats such as Magic Johnson, Oscar Robertson, Jerry Lucas, and Kareem Abdul-Jabbar.

• As a testament to his role as the most vital player within the Thunder organization, Westbrook was offered the biggest guaranteed contract in NBA history, a six-year $233 million deal.

Chapter 7: Westbrook Beyond The Court

Aside from his explosive presence on the court and his team leadership, Russell Westbrook has also become known for his exploits off the court, including his creative fashion sense. He collaborated with Barneys New York in launching the Westbrook XO Barneys New York line in 2014. This collaboration is a fusion of daring designs from Westbrook himself, showcasing his love for bold and bright colors and prints. The inaugural collection featured designs by Naked and Famous, Want Les Essentiels, and Jordan, featuring athletic clothing and streetwear geared towards a younger, fashion-forward market. Westbrook has also partnered with Marcelo Burlon County of Milan, Del Toro, and Globe-Trotter for other pieces.

It has been said that Westbrook never wears an outfit twice, and he has certainly made a name for himself as a fashion icon. In an interview on the Ellen Degeneres Show, Westbrook revealed that he only wears an outfit one time and then donates it to Goodwill. The NBA star is not shy about experimenting with bold, vivacious, out-of-the-box prints, colors and outfits that tend to break current rules of style. His very unique personal look has indeed made him an influencer and fashion guru among his followers.

Westbrook is also big on eyewear, and he co-owns Westbrook Frames, a company selling luxury eyewear designed for high-end sports and fashion aficionados. The eyewear features collections that blend the best and the hippest in sports and fashion. According to Marc Beckman, a co-owner of Westbrook Frames and the star's fashion marketing agent, the idea came about when Westbrook's audacious eyewear during post-game interviews, particularly his red frames with no lenses which he wore in 2012, captured the attention of fans and writers alike. Beckman said that getting Westbrook personally involved in the eyewear market became one of their top priorities, and they enlisted the help of Selima Optique to make the process more effective.

"Being that Russell was the one who created this eyewear trend in the NBA, it was important for us to give him the opportunity to own an equity position, and to be the first out in the category of all the players in the NBA," according to Beckman.

Westbrook Frames has partnered with the NBA in creating an eyewear series featuring frames for at least 30 teams initially, with plans for designs for all teams to be made available. Among the initial frames were designs for the Cleveland Cavaliers, Los Angeles Lakers, Boston Celtics, Miami Heat, New York Knicks, Los Angeles Clippers, and Brooklyn Nets. Westbrook Frames also partnered with the NBA in creating an All-Star Series in 2015.

Westbrook has ongoing fashion partnerships with True Religion, LVMH/Zenith Watches, Kings & Jaxs, and Jordan Brand, extending his influence beyond the arena and establishing him as one of his generation's icons in clothing.
Westbrook has even tried his hand at underwear modelling. In 2013, he was asked to model a series of stylish men's underwear for Kings & Jaxs. According to him, "I have always loved fashion, so working with Kings & Jaxs was a natural fit as we both have a fearless and creative approach to style." The brand was picked up by major retailers such as Saks Fifth Avenue and Nordstrom. But beyond being an NBA superstar and a fashion influencer, Westbrook is using his popularity and influence to have a positive and lasting impact on the world. Westbrook is actively involved in several charitable causes and organizations, including the Russell Westbrook Why Not? Foundation, which he started in 2012.
The Foundation aims to inspire young children and empower them to aim for more by asking the question, "Why not?" while instilling the values of hard work and determination. The idea for the Russell Westbrook Why Not? Foundation came from Westbrook and his brother's own experience as children when they were taught to ask, "Why not?" whenever there was something they were told they could not achieve.

Since 2012, the Foundation has supported various community-based educational and family service programs at the grassroots level. Westbrook has also organized basketball camps and bowling tournaments for children being assisted by the Foundation.

Aside from his own organization, Westbrook has also supported other charities such as NBA Cares and Greater Than AIDS. He frequently appears in television spots for NBA Cares and is one of the most visible supporters of the program. NBA Cares uses the league's worldwide reach to focus attention on different social responsibility programs, tackling issues in the United States and globally.

NBA Cares partners with youth and family-focused programs such as the Special Olympics, Boys and Girls Clubs of America, UNICEF, Make-A-Wish Foundation, YMCA of the USA, Share Our Strength, and GLSEN. Since its inception in 2005, NBA Cares has raised more than $270 million, rendered 3.5 million hours of service, and built 995 building projects in communities all over the world.
In his own foundation and his support of other worthy causes, Westbrook is utilizing his high profile and celebrity status to encourage the next generation and help children realize their potential, while also inspiring others to help in shaping the future of the world through education and community-based programs.

Chapter Summary

• Russell Westbrook has become known as a fashion icon because of his unique style, and he has used this fashion sense to partner with major retail brands and produce his own clothing line.

• Westbrook also has his own eyewear company, Westbrook Frames, which features designs blending sports and fashion.

• Westbrook has also tried modelling for underwear brand Kings & Jaxs.

• The Russell Westbrook Why Not? Foundation was established in 2012 and aims to inspire children to dream big and reach for their dreams.

• Westbrook supports other causes such as NBA Cares and Greater Than AIDS.

Chapter 8: What's Next For Westbrook?

Russell Westbrook is, without a doubt, the cornerstone of Oklahoma City basketball at the moment. While the Thunder boast a solid supporting cast that makes the team a reliable playoff contender, it is obvious that the future of the team rises and falls with Westbrook, hence the organization's decision to offer him a massive contract that ensures he will stay with OKC.

Despite the departure of Kevin Durant, Westbrook has managed to lead Oklahoma City in an increasingly competitive Western Conference, and now with the addition of marquee stars Paul George and Carmelo Anthony, Westbrook and the Thunder remain very much in the thick of things even with the dominance of the Golden State Warriors and the Houston Rockets.

The new Big Three of OKC will have to live up to a lot of hype surrounding their challenge to the throne of the Warriors. Many sports insiders and experts believe that while Westbrook, George, and Anthony are worthy opponents, they will likely still have difficulty dethroning the Warriors out west, with Steph Curry, Klay Thompson, and the rest of the crew already playing together for several seasons. The addition of Kevin Durant was almost picture-perfect; from the get-go, it seemed like he was destined to play with the Splash Brothers, jiving with Steve Kerr's system almost instantly.

However, if George and Anthony decide to stick around with Westbrook for more than just a year or two, things could look quite different come the 2019-20 NBA season, as Thompson might look for other options and Curry moves past his prime. One thing is for sure, Oklahoma City Thunder fans will expect to at least have Westbrook in their corner for the foreseeable future, and now it is up to the organization to plan strategic moves that will ensure he will have a group that can match his skill and on-court prowess as the Thunder seek NBA dominance.

For as long as Westbrook remains with the Thunder, the team's future is stable because it gives the team at least a fair chance of surviving the Wild West. Westbrook knew his decision to stay with Oklahoma City, a relatively small NBA market with a passionate following, would affect decisions and careers for many of the other guys on the squad. Had Westbrook chosen to take his talents elsewhere, there would have been no reason for Oklahoma City to keep Enes Kanter, Mitch McGary, or Josh Heustis. Without Westbrook, it would not even have made sense to go after Anthony or George, two stars who are not getting any younger.

Westbrook's prime playing years in the NBA will be with the Thunder, and this should be enough to keep basketball fans interested to see how the dreamer from Long Beach, California will continue to etch his place in history. Of course, he has already established himself alongside many of the game's greatest, with his numerous triple-double records and his ability to score, defend, and pass reminiscent to legends of years past. He is the league's Most Valuable Player, and rightfully so, considering what he is doing for his team.

But any player knows that individual accolades and records pale in comparison to that ultimate goal: the NBA title. This has eluded Westbrook to this day and remains that one missing piece in an already storied career. The talent of Westbrook as a player is unmistakable, and decades from now, basketball lovers will still be talking about his many accomplishments as one of the most exciting individuals ever to make it to the NBA stage. Will a championship also be in those discussions? For now, we have to wait and see.

Chapter Summary

• Where Westbrook goes, so does the Thunder, as he is the main man for Oklahoma City basketball.

• The addition of Paul George and Carmelo Anthony to the Thunder line-up should make them a more formidable presence in the Western Conference.

• The Golden State Warriors remain the biggest obstacles to Westbrook and the Thunder's championship dreams.

• Westbrook already has an impressive NBA career, but a championship ring would be the ultimate prize for one of the greatest players in NBA history.

Conclusion

Once again, thank you for taking the time to read this book about Russell Westbrook. His story is one that is interesting to read about whether you are a basketball follower or not, or even if you are rooting for a different team. Westbrook has risen above personal circumstances, several injuries, big team changes, and other obstacles, and has continued to impress everyone around the league with his brand of basketball.

His own foundation's slogan, "Why Not?", clearly has empowered him in his personal life as he keeps on reaching for greater heights despite difficulties and uncertainties around him. It is also an inspiration to know that despite the success he is enjoying today, he remains committed to giving back and sharing his life and his blessings with others around him, using his position as a globally-recognized ambassador of the game of basketball to shine the light on important issues, including education and community service.

The life story of Westbrook is far from over. In fact, impressive as it may already be, perhaps we have only seen the first few chapters of what looks to be another story that will be talked about for decades to come. How Westbrook will live up to the expectations and continue to shine as a basketball player, an entrepreneur, a fashion designer, and a community supporter will truly be exciting to watch in the coming years.